HIS FINEST DAYS

Ten Sermons For Holy Week And The Easter Season

BY ROBERT L. ALLEN

C.S.S. Publishing Co., Inc.
Lima, Ohio

HIS FINEST DAYS

Library of Congress Cataloging-in-Publication Data

Allen, Robert L., 1946-
His finest days — ten sermons for Holy Week and the Easter serason / by Robert L. Allen.
78 p. 14 by 21.5 cm.
ISBN 1-55673-603-7
1. Holy-Week sermons. 2. Eastertide — Sermons. 3. Sermons, American. I. Title.
BV4298.A455 1993
252-.62—dc20 92-40876
CIP

9323 / ISBN 1-55673-603-7 PRINTED IN U.S.A.

This book is dedicated
to the people of
Wesley United Methodist Church

Table Of Contents

Preface 7

Palm Sunday 9
The Impossibility Of Neutrality
Mark 11:1-11

Maundy Thursday 16
When Life Closes In
Matthew 26:17-30; 36-50

Good Friday 23
The Paradox Of The Cross
Mark 15:20-25; 1 Corinthians 1:18-25

Easter Sunday 30
An Empty Tomb
Matthew 28:1-10

The Second Sunday Of Easter 37
Let Me See Your Hands
John 20:19-29

The Third Sunday Of Easter 44
Encounter With A Stranger
Luke 24:13-35

The Fourth Sunday Of Easter 52
Breakfast In Galilee
John 21:1-14

The Fifth Sunday Of Easter 59
Do You Love Me?
John 21:15-19

The Sixth Sunday Of Easter 65
One More Thing
Matthew 28:16-20

Ascension Sunday 72
When God Disappears
Acts 1:6-11

Preface

It would not be an exaggeration to say that the finest days in the life of Jesus were his last days. It was during these last days that Jesus struggled with his emotions. He struggled with his mission. He struggled with his direction in life. He struggled with his destiny.

The finest days in the life of Jesus began when he made his triumphant march into Jerusalem. This event was a pivotal point in his ministry. Up until this point, he had been merely an irritation to the Jewish religious establishment. But the triumphant march into Jerusalem opened a new dimension of conflict with the religious authorities.

It was during these days that a new sense of urgency came into the messages of Jesus. Each day, from the Palm Sunday entry to the resurrection event to the Ascension experience, called forth the best that was within him. As we make our journey with him through his final days, I believe that we will also be convinced that these were his finest days.

Robert L. Allen

Palm Sunday
Mark 11:1-11

The Impossibility Of Neutrality

This last week I spent the better part of three days involved in interviews with the Board of Ministry. It was our responsibility to interview men and women in the United Methodist Church. Those being interviewed ranged from their mid-twenties up to a woman who was 68 years old and will be ordained as a deacon at annual conference.

During the interviews, we examined the theological beliefs of the candidates. We listened to tapes of their sermons. We asked a lot of personal questions about their lives; which is a nice way of saying that we were being a little bit nosey about their personal lives and human foibles. We did our best to determine if each candidate would be a credit to the ordained ministry of the church.

Finally, after we had exhaustive interviews with the candidates, they would leave the room and we would discuss their strengths and their weaknesses. Often, the debate would be long and emotional. We would vacillate on certain candidates as we rode the fence trying to determine if we were for or against them. We were torn between accepting and rejecting them.

However, the time of decision came. We could no longer ride the fence and remain neutral. We had to make a choice.

We had to make a decision. It was impossible to remain neutral and we had to vote "yes" or "no" on a candidate's fitness to be a United Methodist minister.

Palm Sunday dramatized in unforgettable fashion the impossiblity of being neutral regarding Jesus. When we read and think about Jesus riding through the Holy City, we usually think about what that event meant to Jesus. Today, we are thinking not only about what it meant to Jesus, but also what it meant to Jerusalem. If only Jesus had stayed away from Jerusalem, what a relief! The city as a whole did not want to accept him. The city as a whole did not want to crucify him. To be honest, I believe that the city as a whole would have dodged the issue about Jesus if they could have. After all, why did they have to make a decision that would split the city wide open?

Look at what happened on that first Palm Sunday. We are mistaken if we think everyone was pleased to see Jesus. Of course, there were those who were excited to see Jesus. They welcomed him with palm branches. They laid their coats in his path. They shouted, "Hosanna!" as he rode by on the back of a donkey. But, there were others in the crowd who cared nothing at all about Jesus. The merchants were there hawking their wares. They enjoyed the large crowd that Jesus attracted, but they probably cared nothing for him. The religious leaders were in the crowd. The proud Pharisees and the greedy Sadducees stood there with their arms folded and whispered about what a nuisance Jesus was, coming to Jerusalem in such a manner during this holy season. And there were the Romans who watched to see if Jesus was a threat to their authority. Accepting Jesus was preposterous, crucifying him was distasteful. They simply wished to side-step any decision having to do with Jesus.

Just as those who were present when Jesus marched into Jerusalem found it difficult to remain neutral about Jesus, so do we. Human nature being what it is, Jesus is still disturbing almost 2,000 years later. We talk about his love and we call him glorious names, but there is something about him that is upsetting. So often, we are made miserable by the necessity of choosing either for him or against him.

If you have never felt that way about Jesus, I suspect that you have never taken him seriously. Life would be easier if the ideas of Jesus didn't force us to choose. And we must decide! It is impossible to be neutral when we are confronted with the ideas of Jesus.

I. It Is Impossible To Be Neutral When It Comes To Jesus' Ideas About Truth.

Why is truth so hard to find? Why is truth so elusive? So obscure? So hidden that only with great difficulty can we find it? Jesus was a revealer of truth. He came into this world and revealed the truth about life, about the infinite value of each person and about goodwill and brotherhood for all people.

Jesus was a revealer of eternal truth and this presents us with forced decisions. For or against, we must make decisions. We cannot remain neutral. We must take sides.

So often, we like to side-step issues and try to remain neutral. But, there comes a time when we must make a decision about what we believe.

One police officer told me that he has always been troubled by parents who try to force their children to do something by threatening them with the police. This tends to make children afraid of the police even in a time of danger. However, the way to handle this type of situation was revealed when he was eating lunch in a cafe with another officer.

A woman in a nearby booth was trying to get her son to eat his meal and said to her little boy in a loud voice, "Jimmy, if you don't eat those green beans, that policeman over there will come and take you to jail."

The officer heard that and he promptly got up and walked over to the five-year-old boy who has being scolded. He reached out and tousled the boy's head and said, "Jimmy, I am six foot two and weigh 200 pounds. I can't stand green beans and I never eat them either."

Just as that officer confirmed the truth that the police are not our enemies, but our friends and helpers, Jesus is the revealer of eternal truth and this finds confirmation in the fact that others have said some of the same things Jesus said. The Golden Rule of Jesus, "Do unto others what you would have them do unto you," is not original with Jesus. Hundreds of years before Jesus, the Jewish law said, "What is hurtful to yourself do not do to your fellow man." Buddha said, "Hurt not others with what pains yourself." Hinduism says, "Do naught to others which if done to thee, would cause thee pain." Strangely, there are some who believe that this lack of originally detracts from Jesus' uniqueness. But, to the contrary, when eternal truth, waiting to be revealed, breaks through the clouds and is accepted as truth by many, that simply confirms the revelation.

So, long before Copernicus, Pythagoras guessed that the earth circled the sun, long before Columbus, the viking, Eric the Red, discovered America, long before Martin Luther, Tyndale and others rebelled and protested abuses within the Catholic Church.

Nevertheless, it is Copernicus the world remembers as the founder of modern astronomy. It is Columbus the world credits with discovering America. It is Martin Luther the world remembers as the first leader of the Protestant Reformation and it is Jesus Christ who forces the issue on us now, saying, "This is the everlasting truth!" Are you for it or against it?

If Jesus were simply another religious leader, we could sidestep him. But, the truth he revealed makes it impossible to ignore him.

II. It Is Impossible To Be Neutral When It Comes To Jesus' Ideas About The Sacredness Of Life

One of the unique things about Jesus is that he taught that people are sacred. Every person who breathes a breath of life is valuable. There may be times when you do not feel like it.

There are many times when you do not act like it, but your life is important to God. Your life is sacred simply because that is the way God made life.

The sacredness and value of life was revealed when Jesus said, "For God so loved the world that he gave his only begotten Son, that whosoever believeth in him should not perish, but have everlasting life." Jesus was teaching that you are important because your life is sacred. It is so sacred that God came into this life through Christ for you.

Some time ago, I conducted a funeral service for a young man about 20 years old who had taken his own life. The family lived in another city and when they came back to this city for the funeral, they called me and asked if I would officiate at the service. I was glad to be able to help them and be with them.

When I tell this, I am not trying to make myself sound like a hero. I believe I only did what you would have done. At the conclusion of the service, I was standing beside the casket when the man's 22-year-old sister came up and began to cry. As she stood beside her brother's casket, she whispered, "I hate you for doing this!"

She looked up and realized I had heard her. She was embarrassed. I simply put my arms around her shoulder and said, "Susan, there's nothing wrong with what you said. Of course you hate him for doing this to himself, to you and to your family."

Now, did she really mean she hated her brother? Of course not! She was saying, "I love you so much. I don't know why you did this to yourself, and to me, to Mom and Dad and to everyone who loves you."

She was simply asking, "Why?" Every life is sacred and somewhere deep inside of us we know that to be true. Jesus proclaimed the sacredness of life. I am sure of that! The sacredness and inherent worth of each life is something about which we must decide — are we for or against?

A few weeks ago, on one of those cold, cold nights, I drove down a street which ran behind a large grocery store. As I drove by the large garbage canister, I saw some movement in the shadows. I slowed down and looked a little closer. There was a woman and two small children — the oldest not more than 10 or 11 years old. They were scavenging for discarded canned goods in that garbage dumpster. These people were hungry and searching for food. These people did not live in some third world country. These people were right here in the state of Oklahoma. These people were right here in our own community.

I believe that we are confronted with a personal decision about the value and importance of each life. We cannot remain neutral. We cannot ignore the question. We must decide — for or against — that every life is sacred and valuable.

III. It Is Impossible To Be Neutral When It Comes To Jesus' Ideas About God.

Every person has his or her God. You may give your life to money, power, ambition, alcohol, lust or what have you, but all of us have our gods. We are born worshipers, always giving our lives to something. The God-question is inescapable. We cannot avoid it. We cannot be neutral about it. We either choose Jesus' God or some other. For or against the God and Father of our Lord Jesus Christ — on that issue no convenient fence exists where we can sit undecided.

Whenever an individual faced Jesus, he or she was confronted with the God-question. Zacchaeus, the tax collector, was confronted by Jesus. He could not remain neutral. Jesus wanted a yes or a no for an answer. Would he or would he not make restitution for his ill-gotten gains? Would he or would he not clean up his life? Would he or would he not straighten out his life? Everyone who Jesus encountered, he refused to permit to ride the fence and be neutral. He faced them and confronted them with the need to decide. He confronted the woman of Samaria and her mishandling of sex. He confronted Nicodemus about the need to be born again. He confronted the Jews with their race prejudice against the Samaritans.

These and many others Jesus faced with a forced decision — will you or won't you? They would have loved to stay neutral, but Jesus forced them to decide on the God-question. They had to choose for or against.

And you have to choose!

You are confronted today and every day with the God-question.

You will either accept Jesus Christ or reject him!

What will you decide?

Prayer: O God, on this Palm Sunday, give us the courage to choose the way of Jesus Christ. In his name, Amen.

Maundy Thursday
Matthew 26:17-30; 36-50

When Life Closes In

David was a young man in his early 30s and seemed to have everything going his way. He was a successful businessman. He owned a sales and service-oriented business. He owned an entertainment business and he owned an apartment complex.

Besides being successful in business, he was happily married. He had a wife, two children and a big Irish setter that had its own pet chicken. Wherever that Irish setter went, you would see people stop and stare because there would be a Rhode Island Red riding on his back.

David seemed to have it made in life. He was successful in business. He had a happy family life. He had everything going his way. Then, a routine medical examination turned up something very serious — a brain tumor.

I went to the hospital to see him shortly before his surgery. We talked about the things you would expect a young man to be concerned about just prior to undergoing surgery to remove a brain tumor. We talked about his family. We talked about his wife and two chidlren. We talked about his fear of dying.

As we sat there in that hospital room and talked, David stared out the window and looked at the skyline of the city off in the distance. Occasionally, he would use a kleenex to wipe the tears as they trickled down his cheeks. Then, in a voice that was choked with emotion, he looked back toward me and said, "I've never felt this way before. It just seems that life is closing in on me."

Jesus must have felt that life was closing in on him on that Thursday of his final week. The triumphant welcome he had received on Sunday and his angry outburst on Monday driving the money-changers out of the temple had caused the religious leaders to begin plotting how to dispose of Jesus. The teachings and attitude of Jesus made him dangerous to the religious leaders. There is nothing that is as cold and intolerant of the opinions of others as the mindset of fanatical religious leaders who feel they must protect their faith from the heresy of a different opinion.

In this modern era, we have the equivalent of the narrow minded, fanatical Pharisees. They are prevalent in every religion and they can clearly be seen in the current controversy surrounding the book, *The Satanic Verses,* by Salman Rushdie. Those who close their minds and seek the death of another are not pious examples of faith, but evil incarnate.

The religious leaders plotting and planning the death of Jesus were not doing the work of God. They were lost, confused souls who were trying to protect their comfortable existence from the threat of One who seemed to be closer to God than they were. He was a threat and they would have to have him killed.

Jesus did not have his head buried in the sand. He knew that life was closing in on him. He was aware of the dangers and the confrontations which were only a few hours away. Jesus longed for more time. There were many things he still wanted to teach. There were many things he still wanted to do. But time had run out and life was closing in on him.

At one time or another, life closes in on all of us and the experience is especially difficult. Perhaps someone is terribly ill, and we do everything we can for them. We hope and pray that person will get well, but he does not. And it seems like life closes in on us.

There may come a time when it seems like our world comes to an end. Something we hoped and prayed would never happen becomes a reality and it feels like life is closing in on us. Perhaps, someone we love very much no longer loves us. This feels like death and it is — the death of a relationship. It hurts! It hurts deeply and it feels like life is closing in on us. Perhaps, our sins and our guilt begin eating away at our insides. No one else may know about our sins and failures, but we know and we feel unworthy, sick and lost. Our life on the inside of our hearts and minds is a mess of guilt and shame and it seems like life is closing in on us with a vice-grip. What do we do when this happens? When life closes in, what do we do? Do we fight back? Do we throw up our hands and quit? What do we do when life closes in on us?

When we look at Thursday during the last week for Jesus, life was definitely closing in on him. Today, I want to suggest some steps you can take when life seems to be closing in on you. The ideas I suggest are really the steps Jesus took.

I. When Life Was Closing In, Jesus Sought Fellowship With His Friends.

In that hour when doubts and fears were crowding in on Jesus, he sought some quiet fellowship with his disciples as they celebrated the Feast of the Passover. They were aware of the dangers in Jerusalem, but it was important to celebrate the Passover in the Holy City. Quietly, probably walking in groups of two or three so as not to draw attention to their gathering, they walked along the cobblestone streets to a house with an upper room where they would share a meal. It was here in this intimate fellowship with his disciples that Jesus sought some peace and comfort when life was closing in on him.

This is a reaction which seems to make sense. When we are desperate and life seems to be getting us down, we like to be with people with whom we are comfortable, with whom we love and with whom we care about. When life seems to be closing in, we can find some comfort and peace in fellowship with our friends. People do not have to say much in these moments, they just need to be people we care about and who care about us. There is nothing more reassuring than being with people we care about when life is closing in on us.

A few years ago, a couple invited me out to lunch. I knew them as a couple who attended our church, but I did not know them very well. As we were eating lunch, they told me that they were going to get marreid and wanted to know if I would officiate at the wedding ceremony.

I told them I would. They were a delightful couple and I asked them how they met. "We met at the Special Olympics," the woman said.

Intrigued at where they met, I asked them to tell me about the Special Olympics. They spoke with a great deal of tenderness about helping young athletes struggle to do things that you and I do without a second thought. Things like jumping, throwing a ball or running took a great deal of effort on the part of these young people who had special handicaps. The reward for these young people was not in winning, but in participating.

I looked at the woman and asked, "What is your most memorable experience in working with the Special Olympics?"

She smiled and said, "It was the finals in the 100-yard dash. Most of the other events were over and everyone was watching this event. The athletes were crouched in the starting position waiting for the starter's gun. With the sound of the gun, the athletes were off with their eyes fixed on the finish line. However, about 50 yards down the track, one runner stumbled and fell. The three other runners stopped and went back to help the fourth. They helped him up. They brushed the gravel and dirt from his scraped and bleeding knees and then walking four abreast, with their arms around each other, they walked to the finish line together."

We often find ourselves battered and bruised in life and lying flat on the ground. We are wounded. We are facing a dark period in life. Doubt and fear seem to be overwhelming us. Life is closing in on us and we don't know where to turn or what to do.

If we follow the example of Jesus, we will seek fellowship with our friends. They may not make our problems disappear, but we will discover a comfort and a peace growing in our hearts and our lives because we know that someone cares.

Do you feel like life is closing in on you?

Do you feel like you are facing some kind of crisis in your life because everything seems to be so overwhelming?

Do you feel like life has knocked you down and left you battered and bruised?

Then look at what Jesus did! He was running out of time. He was facing the cross of Calvary. He felt life was closing in on him. And he sought the fellowship of his friends. So can you!

II. When Life Was Closing In, Jesus Sought Fellowship With God.

Catch the setting in your mind. Jesus and his disciples had just celebrated the last supper in the upper room. Judas had slipped off to betray Jesus for only 30 pieces of silver. Jesus knew what was lying ahead. Life was closing in on him and he wanted to go to the Garden of Gethsemane. Quietly, they slipped out of the Upper Room. It was almost midnight as they walked past the lower pool and through the fountain gate. They moved up the hill toward the garden. Jesus turned and looked back toward the city. A few lights twinkled across the city that was mostly asleep, the spire of the temple, tipped with gold was glistening in the moonlight. In the distance, Jesus could hear a Roman sentry calling his watch. Jesus walked on a little way in the darkness alone. He wanted to be alone where he could pray and seek fellowship with God. Life was closing in on him and he knelt in prayer.

The scriptures tell us that Jesus, "... being in agony ... prayed most earnestly, and his sweat become like great drops of blood falling down upon the ground." Jesus knew what was before him. He knew that the hatred of men and women was about to nail him to a cross. He was grappling with fear in that garden as he prayed: "Father, if it be possible, let this cup pass from me."

I am firmly convinced that Jesus knew what was before him as he prayed in the garden. He knew that life was closing in and he was reaching out his hand for the hand of God. He was seeking fellowship with God and the darkness could not overwhelm him.

Helen Steiner Rice used an old Danish fable to write a poem she titled: "The Legend of the Spider and Silken Thread Held in God's Hand." It is a good poem and it makes a good point. She wrote:

There's an old Danish Legend
with a lesson for us all,
Of an ambitious spider
and his rise and fall.
Who wove his sheer web
with intricate care
As it hung suspended
somewhere in mid-air.
Then in soft, idle luxury
he feasted each day
On the small, foolish insects
he enticed as his prey.
Growing ever more arrogant
and smug all the while
He lived like a "king"
in self-satisfied style.
And gazing one day
at the sheer strand suspended.
He said, "I don't need this,"
so he recklessly rended
The strand that had held
his web in its place.

And with sudden swiftness
that web crumbled in space —
And that was the end
of the spider who grew
So arrogantly proud
that he no longer knew
That it was the strand
that reached down from above
Like the chord of God's grace
and his infinite love
That links our lives
to the great unknown.
For a man cannot live
or exist on his own —
And this old legend
with simplicity told
Is a moral as true
as the legend is old. —
Don't sever the "lifeline"
that links you to
The Father in Heaven
who cares about you.

When life is closing in on you, reach out your hand to the hand of God. When you are linked to the "Father in Heaven," when you are in fellowship with God, you will discover the strength and the faith to face whatever comes your way in life.

Are you reaching out your hand to God? God is already reaching out to you. Will you reach out to him?

Prayer: O God, as life closes in on us, give us the wisdom to reach out to God who is already reaching out to us. In Jesus' name. Amen.

Good Friday
Mark 15:20-25; 1 Corinthians 1:18-25

The Paradox Of The Cross

It was a few years ago that I spoke of the little cross in my pocket. Since that Sunday, people not only in this church, but people all across this state who watch our services on television, have asked for one of these little crosses to carry in their pockets or purse. It would be a mistake to think of this little cross as possessing magical powers, or supposedly bringing luck like a rabbit's foot or guiding us to say just the right words at just the right time. There is no magical quality or guidance in this cross. It is simply a reminder that Jesus Christ was crucified on a cross.

A woman in Arkansas, Verna Thomas, wrote a little poem explaining what it means to carry a little cross around in her pocket. She wrote:

I carry a cross in my pocket,
A simple reminder to me.
Of the fact that I am a Christian
No matter where I may be.
This little cross is not magic,
Nor is it a good luck charm;
It isn't meant to protect me
From any physical harm.

It is not for identification,
For all the world to see . . .
It is simply an understanding
Between my Savior and me.
When I put my hand in my pocket
To bring out a coin or a key,
The cross is there to remind me
Of all that he's done for me.
It reminds me, too, to be thankful
For my blessings day by day;
And to strive to serve him better
In all I do or say.
It is also a daily reminder
Of the peace and comfort I share
With all who know my Master,
and give themselves to his care.
So I carry a cross in my pocket
Reminding me, no one but me,
That Jesus Christ is Lord of my life
If only I'll let him be.

Across the years, the symbol of the cross has become a symbol of our faith. You will find the cross atop the steeples of many churches. You will find the cross worn as a necklace around the necks of many people. You will find the cross in every nation and every race throughout the world as a symbol of the Christian faith. And this is really a paradox because the cross was once a symbol of suffering and shame.

You cannot read the scriptures without getting the clear impression that Jesus knew the possibility of a cross was before him. The idea of the cross frightened him. The cross was the cruelest form of a slow agonizing death ever created to kill another. The cross was intended to humiliate as well as slowly kill its victim. Jesus knew about the cross and he prayed: "O God, let this cup pass from me . . ."

Jesus knew about the possibility of the cross and on Friday of his last week, it became a reality. He went through the mockery of a trial. He listened as the crowd began to chant,

"Crucify, Crucify, Crucify." He endured the savage beating of the whip with little metal fragments sewed into the tips of the leather that ripped his back into a bloody pulp. He stumbled under the heavy weight of the cross as he walked along the Via Dolorosa toward a skull-shaped hill called Golgotha. He felt the pain as the rusty nails were driven through his hands and his feet. There was agony as these nails tore at his shredded flesh when the cross was lifted up and dropped with a thud into the hole prepared for it.

This is the paradox of the cross. There is no question that the cross was an emblem of suffering and shame and humiliation. According to the Apostle Paul, the cross was a stumbling block to the Jews and foolishness to the Greeks. But, somewhere along the way, the cross has become the greatest single symbol which unites the followers of Jesus Christ.

Today, as we look at the paradox of the cross, there are three things which I think are important.

I. The Paradox Of The Cross Is That It Was A Crushing Defeat For Jesus, Yet It Helps To Understand That Our Sins Do Not Separate Us From God.

On this Good Friday, throughout all of Christendom, we are remembering one of the most colossal failures in history. Jesus had failed. Jesus was crucified. Jesus was dead.

And this is the paradox. Nearly 2,000 years later, one of the most profound things we can say about the cross is that it tells us there is not anything in this world which can separate you from God. You may sin and that sin may leave you feeling guilty, ashamed and cut off from God.

When Adam ate the forbidden fruit in the Garden of Eden, he had sinned. The guilt of his sin made him feel like he had fallen away from God. He was so ashamed of that sin that he went and hid. When God called out to him and asked why he was hiding, Adam said, "I was afraid and tried to hide myself."

Sin makes us feel guilty and ashamed. Sometimes, we are so overwhelmed with a sense of our own guilt that we want to "hide" ourselves. But, the good news of the gospel is that we do not have to hide ourselves. Our sins do not cut us off from God. Our sins do not separate us from God. The cross of Calvary shows us a God who loves us and forgives us.

There is a story about a teenage boy who walked into a little cafe one day and sat down. It was a small place and the boy said, "I'm hungry, but I don't have any money. If you will give me something to eat, I'll wash dishes or clean your windows."

While the owner was getting a bowl of chili and some crackers, he asked the boy, "Have you been on your own very long?"

The boy ate his bowl of chili and told his story as he ate. He told of an argument with his father and how he left home. He had been on his own now for six months — six long, tough months.

The owner of the cafe noticed the boy's bowl was empty, so he dipped him another bowl of chili. Then he said, "Son, your story is very familiar. My son and I got mad at each other a few months back. I said a lot of things in anger and he got mad and left. He's been gone for months and I have no idea where he is. This little cafe isn't much, but I own it! I would hand over the keys this very minute to have my son back home."

Then the man looked at the boy and said, "I imagine your father feels pretty much like I do. He can't take back the things he said in the past, but he still cares about you. What I'm trying to say to you is, Why don't you go back home? I'm sure he loves you enough to try again."

The paradox of the cross is that it seemed like a crushing defeat, a devastating failure, a colossal triumph of evil over good that day they crucified Jesus. But, the paradox is that defeat has been reversed. It is because of the cross that we know we can go home to God. We may have sinned, but God still loves us. We may be filled with guilt, but we can be forgiven.

We may be ashamed of our sins, but our sins do not separate us from God. There is nothing that stands between us and God, except the cross of Jesus Christ. We can go home again. There is nothing that stands between us and God, except the cross of Jesus Christ. We can go home again.

II. The Paradox Of The Cross Is That It Was A Tragic And Cruel Thing, But The Cross Helps Us See Hope.

Look at the cross in its stark horror. What happened there was tragic and cruel. It was an act of barbarism which clearly shows what we are capable of doing to another. Jesus' religious leaders had rejected him as a traitor. The soldiers had spit on him. Pilate had washed his hands of him. He was so alone at the cross of Calvary that he cried out, "My God, my God, why hast thou forsaken me."

And this is the paradox! The cross was a tragic and cruel way to die, but Jesus could look beyond the cross. Jesus could look beyond the suffering and pain. Jesus could see hope on the horizon. And it is this hope of Jesus conquering death which gives us hope. Because of Jesus Christ, we can see hope beyond the crosses in our lives.

A few years ago, a man dropped by my office to see me. I did not know him, although he claimed to be a member of this church. He was one of those members whose name was on our roll, but was not active. In fact, as soon as he was seated, he said, "I just thought I ought to come by and meet the preacher."

I laughed and said, "Well, I'm glad you did. But there must be something on your mind. What is it?"

He told me that he had been undergoing a series of tests at the doctor's office and all of the indications were that he had some malignant tumors and he would be having surgery the next morning. We talked about his surgery. We talked about the possibility that the tumors were malignant. We talked about the fear he was experiencing. But, even more important we talked about one who could help him look beyond the fears of the moment and see hope out there on the horizon.

The paradox of the cross is that it was a tragic and cruel way to die, but because of Jesus Christ, there is hope on the horizon. The cross of Calvary tells us there is nothing — not cancer, not heart problems, not AIDS, not fear, not death, nor anything in all of creation that can separate us from God's love in Jesus Christ. We may be hurting. We may be filled with fear. We may be feeling the breath of death breathing on the back of our necks. But, there is hope beyond our crosses. Jesus said, "He that liveth and believeth in me shall never die." This is our eternal hope!

III. Another Paradox Of The Cross Is That The Cross Was The Most Terrible Thing That Could Have Happened To Jesus, Yet It Shows Us What God Is like.

This is really the crowning paradox of all. The cross was a denial of God, a blatant, cruel denial of God, and yet it was supremely the revelation of God. It was God saying, "I am like Jesus Christ." It was God saying, "I love and care about you."

One of my favorite stories, a story I have told many times, comes from the old play, *Green Pastures*. When it played on Broadway, there was the final scene where God and the angel Gabriel were in a room in heaven. Gabriel looks out of the window of heaven and says, "Look, Lord, they're beating him with that whip! Is the time come for me to blow the horn?"

And God says, "No, Gabriel, not yet!"

Again Gabriel looks out the window of heaven and says, "Lord, they're making him carry that cross up the hill by himself! Are you ready for me to blow the horn?"

And God says, "No, Gabriel, not yet!"

"Lord," Gabriel says with excitement in his voice, "they're nailing him to that cross! Surely you want me to blow the horn now?"

And God says, "No, Gabriel, not yet!"

Gabriel shakes his head and he says, "Lord, that's a terrible burden for one man. Why are you letting them do it to him? Why?"

Then, God, who throughout the entire play has had his back to the audience turns and looks directly at every person in the audience and says, "'Caus' I loves them, Gabe! 'Caus' I loves them!"

And this is the paradox of the cross. The crucifixion of Jesus Christ on the cross of Calvary was the most terrible thing that could happen to Jesus. And yet, it is through the cross of Calvary that we come to know what God is like. It is through the cross of Calvary that God is fully revealed. It is through the cross of Calvary that we come to know of God's love.

Have you discovered God's love in your life? You can, by looking at the cross of Calvary!

Prayer: Our gracious heavenly Father, for your love revealed to us in Jesus Christ, we give thanks. In his sacred name. Amen.

Easter Sunday
Matthew 28:1-10

An Empty Tomb

Perhaps you saw the story on the news about a couple who had adopted a little girl when she was only two or three weeks old. They accepted the child into the home. They grew to love the child. They watched her grow and develop. But, for some reason, the little girl didn't grow and develop normally. She is now two-and-one-half years old and the doctors have told these adoptive parents that their little girl is mentally retarded and she will never be the normal child they wanted.

The reason this story made the news is because the adoptive parents no longer want the child. They have sued in court to relinquish their parental rights and return custody of the child to the adoption agency.

When I heard that story on the news, I remembered a couple who were members of a previous church I pastored. They adopted a little boy and when he was about four years old, they wanted to adopt a little girl whom they could love and would be a sister to their son.

After a waiting period, they received a little girl from the adoption agency. She was a beautiful child and they named her Amy. But Amy did not grow or develop as a normal child.

She, too, was diagnosed as having mental handicaps. But, these parents chose to love her and help her develop just as much as she possibly could.

When this family moved to our community, Amy's mother brought her to Sunday school and even helped that class of seven-year-old boys and girls understand Amy's difficulties. And the children responded by accepting Amy and treating her as one of their friends.

That first spring that they lived in our community, the children of that seven-year-old class listened in fascination as their Sunday school teacher told them the story of the first Easter. Since it was a beautiful day, the teacher had come up with a creative plan for her class. She had been saving those panty hose containers that look like large eggs. She had decorated them to look like Easter eggs and she gave each child one and told them they were to go outside and find symbols of new life, put them in the Easter egg and bring them back to the classroom. When everyone returned, they would share what they found.

The children loved the excursion out to the church lawn. They ran and laughed and giggled as they searched for a symbol of new life to put into their egg. When they returned, each child got to open their egg and show what they found. A little girl opened hers and a pretty flower fell out. A little boy opened his and half of a robin egg fell out. Another little boy opened his and the butterfly that he caught in the yard flew out. Then, it was time to open Amy's Easter egg. Amy opened her egg and it was empty. There was nothing inside. The teacher smiled and asked, "Couldn't you find anyting to put in the egg, Amy?"

Amy looked at her teacher and said, "It's empty because the tomb of Jesus is empty."

The message of that first Easter is a message that has echoed across the centuries — the tomb is empty. There is nothing inside except the discarded grave clothes lying there, mute but eloquent evidence that a living organism had come out. The grave clothes lay like the shriveled, cracked shell of a cocoon, left behind when the butterfly had emerged and hoisted its beautiful wings to fly in the sunshine.

Jesus was dead! The Roman soldiers had seen to that. They drove huge nails through his hands and feet. The cry of the pain was expected. The barbarity of the crucifixion made even the hardest person in the crowd cringe in sympathy. Six hours of torture on that cross drained all of his strength and he quietly said, "It is finished . . . Father, into thy hands I commit my Spirit," and he was dead. But, just to make sure, one soldier took his lance and pierced the side of Jesus, and the last remaining drops of blood poured out.

They took him down from the cross and buried him in the borrowed tomb of Joseph of Arimathea. They hastily anointed his body with the burial ointments before the beginning of the Jewish Sabbath at sundown on Friday. They would wait all of Friday night and all day Saturday and not return to the tomb, lest they defile themselves according to Jewish law. However, at the first dawning of light on Sunday morning, they would return to the tomb and finish the anointing of the dead body with oils and ointments.

However, sometime in the early morning hours, just prior to the dawning of a new day, there is a rustling as the breath of God moves through the garden. Jesus rises from that cold, stone slab where he had been laid. He stands for a moment on wounded feet. He catches the strange scents of the tomb with its bandages and spices and then he walks out of that tomb — alive forevermore.

This is the message of Easter that echoes across the centuries. The tomb is empty. Christ has risen! Jesus is alive forevermore.

I don't claim to understand or comprehend the full meaning of Easter. In fact, I doubt if any of us really understand. However, I believe with everything in my being that the first Easter and every Easter since then is the message of an empty tomb.

Today, I want to look at some of the implications of the empty tomb on that first Easter.

I. On That First Easter, The Empty Tomb Was A Surprise.

Implicit in the whole story of that first Easter is that the disciples and followers of Jesus, the religious leaders in Jerusalem and the Roman authorities, never expected to see Jesus again. The resurrection, with its empty tomb, was the last thing anyone expected. When Mary and the other women made their way toward the tomb and discovered the stone rolled away, they were surprised.

When the disciples were told that the tomb was empty, Peter and John ran to investigate because this news surprised them. When the religious leaders of Jerusalem heard of the empty tomb from their guard of soldiers, they were so surprised that they created a story and told the soldiers to say, "... the disciples came during the night and stole his body ..." They tried everything they could think of to silence the news of the empty tomb, but nothing worked.

The empty tomb was not some fantastic idea conjured up by grieving hearts. Nor, was it the result of wishful thinking. The news of the empty tomb had come as a complete shock. It was unexpected. It was bewildering. It was a surprise.

There is recorded in the scripture the amazing change that came over these disciples once they were surprised with the empty bomb. They were not courageous individuals. When Jesus was arrested and crucified, the disciples were fearful for their own lives. Yet, after that first Easter morning, these same men who were so timid, so frightened, so ineffective, were now preaching openly, with no fear of anyone. The empty tomb had so surprised them that it filled them with boldness, courage and power.

The surprising change that happened in their lives is something that can happen in yours. I know it can! I've seen it happen many times.

I know a woman who was married for 25 years and had grown children. Although her marriage had survived for many years, it was not a healthy or happy marriage. In fact, the woman and her boss had been involved in an affair for almost two years.

One Sunday, she came to church and was surprised with the relevance of the gospel to her life. Later, she came by my office and told me she felt God wanted her to change the direction of her life. She didn't know if she could change, but she was going to try. She broke off the affair with her boss. She worked at renewing her relationship with her husband. She became a good, honorable woman trying to live her faith in God.

This is Easter Sunday and that is what I wish for you — a surprise. I want you to find his love when you do not expect it. I want you to find his relationship when you think it is not there. I want you to find Jesus Christ when you are convinced his tomb is empty.

II. On That First Easter, The Empty Tomb Was An Experience Of Joy.

On that first Easter Sunday, Mary Magdalene; Salome, the mother of James and John; and Mary, the mother of Jesus; were up before the light of dawn and were on their way to the tomb where the body of Jesus had been laid. Sorrow and grief still bubbled in their hearts because they had seen Jesus crucified. They were weeping and red-eyed. They had not really slept since Friday. They had no real taste for food. The grieving and the sense of loss simply overwhelmed them.

When they arrived at the tomb, the stone was rolled away and the tomb was empty. They were shocked and thought grave robbers had broken it open. They could not understand what happened or why it happened. Tears flooded their eyes and trickled down their cheeks. Sorrow made their hearts feel as though they were going to break. Their minds were tortured with the shock of Jesus' body missing from the tomb.

Then, they were greeted by the risen Lord who said, "Chairete." The literal meaning of the word is, "Rejoice."

Suddenly, the sorrow gave way to joy when they realized that the empty tomb meant that Jesus was alive.

The first Easter and the empty tomb was an experience of joy for the women and the disciples. I believe that our faith in him is the promise that joy can fill our lives.

Recently, I was in Denver for some meetings. Whenever the meetings were over for the day, I would watch the local news. Like many people in Denver, I became fascinated with a particular news story. It was not a story on the presidential election which captured my attention. It was not a story on the Iran-Contra scandal. It was not a story about the majestic beauty of the Colorado Rockies.

The story which captured my attention and the interest of people all over Colorado, was about a newborn baby that was left on the doorstep of a Catholic convent. Evidently, some mother felt completely inadequate at raising a child and had decided to leave the baby on the doorstep of the convent.

There was one nun who was allowed to meet and talk to the public. She was about 60 years old, but she looked positively radiant as she held the baby and showed her off to the news reporters. One of the reporters asked, "Sister, have you named the baby?"

"Yes," the Sister replied, "We call her 'Joy' because of the joy she has brought into our lives."

In a wonderful way, joy has been brought into each of our lives because of the first Easter. The message of that first Easter proclaims an empty tomb that has rescued us and fills us with the joy of life.

III. On That First Easter, The Empty Tomb Was A Promise That Because Jesus Lives, We Will Live.

This is the real meaning of Easter. No news story will ever be flashed around the world that the mummified body of Jesus has been discovered. We have no embalmed body of Jesus enclosed in glass for all the world to see. All that we have is an empty tomb and the promise of Jesus: "Because I live, you will live."

Several years ago, I was visiting one of my members who was in the hospital. I was a young man, fresh out of seminary and still wet behind the ears as a minister. I was visiting this elderly man and he was extremely ill. He wanted to talk to me, his pastor, about his funeral service and I wanted to talk about anything else — the weather, football, politics, or anything else I could think of.

Finally, I asked him, "Joe, doesn't it bother you? Aren't you frightened?"

He smiled and said, "Robert, I know I'm not going to make it, but I'm not afraid. I have a confession to make. I've taken a peek at the back of the book."

"What do you mean?" I asked.

He said, "You didn't know me 10 years ago when I had my first heart attack. They called it cardiac arrest. I can remember the medical team thinking I was dead. I can also remember the tremendous feeling of being surrounded by God's love. I was revived by the doctors, but ever since that day I have been unafraid to die. I've been there and it doesn't frighten me. I know that one day soon I am going to go to sleep and I believe that when I awaken, I will, once again, be surrounded by God's love."

This is the message of the first Easter and every Easter since. The tomb is empty. Christ is risen. Jesus is alive. And because of this, we too, shall live!

Prayer: O God, help us put our faith in Jesus Christ. Help us to know that we can trust him and his promise, "Because I live, you shall live also." We pray through Jesus Christ, our Lord. Amen.

The Second Sunday Of Easter
John 20:19-29

Let Me See Your Hands

A little boy, growing up in a community where his father served as a Methodist minister was outside playing. He was doing all of the things that a little boy does. He was climbing trees. He was swinging on the swing set and jumping out. He was rolling and playing with his dog. His mother called him for dinner and all of the family gathered at the table. His mother looked at him and said, "Young man, let me see your hands."

There was some rubbing of his hands on his blue jeans before he held his hands up. His mother looked at them and asked, "How many times do I have to tell you that you must wash your hands before you eat? When your hands are dirty, they have germs all over them and you could get sick. After we say the blessing, I want you to march back to the bathroom and wash your hands."

Everyone at the table bowed their heads and the father said the blessing. Then, the little boy got up and headed out of the kitchen. He stopped, then turned and looked at his mother and said, "Jesus and germs! That's all I ever hear around here. Jesus and germs!"

That is a humorous little story, but it does point out the fact that our hands can be an identifying characteristic.

Recently, on one of the television programs that deal with unsolved mysteries, they did a re-enactment of a violent crime. At the end, they indicated that they did not have a description of the criminal. However, there was an unusual tattoo on the back of his hand. The criminal could be identified with the tattoo of a skunk on the back of his right hand.

It is not unusual for people to be identified by their hands. According to the F.B.I., every one of us has a different set of fingerprints. We are all different, yet we can be identified by our hands.

And the same was true for Jesus. On that first Easter, Peter and John gathered with the other disciples in that upper room to talk about the empty tomb and the possibility of the resurrection. As they were talking, Jesus came and stood among them. They were frightened, but Jesus reassured them by showing them his hands and feet. How often had the disciples seen those hands of Jesus touch blind eyes so they could see? How often had they seen his hands bless little children? How often had they seen him reach out hands and lift the cripple up and say, "Walk." They saw the hands of Jesus and they knew that he was resurrected from the dead.

However, two disciples were absent from the upper room. Judas was dead and Thomas had slipped off to be alone in his grief over the crucifixion of Jesus. King George V must have been like Thomas because he said, "If I have to suffer, let me be like a well-bred animal ... Let me go and suffer alone."

Thomas had slipped off alone to grieve the death of Jesus. Consequently, Thomas was not with the other disciples in the upper room when Jesus appeared among them on that first Easter. When the other disciples told Thomas of the resurrection, he refused to believe. Thomas said: "You've all been through a great deal of stress. You were simply hallucinating."

"But it's true!" the disciples said, "It is true!"

And Thomas replied: "I can't believe what you're saying. Unless I see in his hands the print of the nails, I will not believe."

One week later, on the first Sunday after Easter, Thomas received his proof. The disciples, including Thomas, were gathered in the upper room when Jesus appeared in their midst. Jesus knew what was in Thomas' heart and he said: "Thomas, if it's proof you want, look at my hands . . . look where the nails have been."

Thomas was overwhelmed. His skepticism and doubt were gone. He fell to his knees and said: "My Lord and my God."

Fanny Crosby, in one of her hymns wrote:

I shall know him, I shall know him,
And redeemed by his side I shall stand,
I shall know him, I shall know him.
By the print of the nails in his hand.

Today, as we look with Thomas at the hands of Jesus, there are three things which I believe his hands say to us.

I. The Hands Of Jesus Remind Us Of His Suffering.

In our society, we believe that the punishment we give to convicted criminals should not be cruel or inhumane. However, the Romans worked at making their punishment cruel. The victim of a crucifixion literally died a thousand deaths. And so it was with Jesus on the cross. He suffered and died at the hands of the Roman soldiers. Whenever we doubt that suffering, all we have to do is look at his hands. It is his hands which remind us of the suffering he experienced.

I read a story recently about a little boy who sat staring at his mother's hands. Finally, he asked, "Mama, why are your hands so ugly?"

The mother was quiet for a moment. Then, she said, "Jason, one day when you were almost three years old, you were playing in the backyard. Some older boys in the neighborhood were playing with matches in the alley. They built a fire and left it burning when they left. You toddled up to the fire and fell. The flames caught your shirt on fire. I heard you screaming. I rushed out of the house. I beat the flames out with my hands. You were scarcely burned, but my hands were burned and scarred terribly. That's why my hands are so ugly."

The little boy looked up at his mother with a smile on his face and said, "Mama, your hands aren't ugly, they're beautiful."

A poet, looking at the hands of Jesus, wrote:

They nailed those beautiful, blessed hands
To the cruel, bitter cross,
And there in agony untold,
He bore our shame and loss.
Beautiful hands of Jesus!
I hope someday to see.
Those wonderful, loving, nail-scarred hands
That were pierced on Calvary.

It is the hands of Jesus which remind us that the cross of Calvary was no picnic. Jesus went to that cross and suffered. Isaiah wrote of the Messiah, "He was wounded for our transgressions; he was bruised for our iniquities." Whenever we doubt that Jesus suffered at the cross, all we have to do is look at his hands. The print of the nails will remind us that "He was wounded for our transgressions."

II. The Hands Of Jesus Remind Us Of His Love.

I read a story by Leslie Flynn who told of a small boy being raised in a frontier city by his grandmother. One night the house catches on fire. The grandmother, trying to rescue the boy who was asleep in the bedroom upstairs, is overcome by the smoke and dies in the fire.

This frontier city doesn't have much of a fire department. A crowd gathers around the house and they hear a small boy crying out for help. The lower floor is a wall of flames and no one seems to know what to do. Suddenly, a man pushes through the crowd and begins climbing an iron drainage pipe which runs to the roof. The pipe is hot from the fire, but he makes it to a second floor window. The man crawls through the window and locates the boy. With the crowd cheering encouragement, the man climbs back down the hot iron pipe with the boy on his back and his arms around his neck.

A few weeks later, a public meeting was held to determine in whose custody the boy would be placed. Each person wanting the child would be allowed to make a brief statement. The first man said, "I have a farm and would give the boy a good home. He would grow up on the farm and learn a trade."

The second person to speak was the local school teacher. She said, "I am a school teacher and I would see to it that he received a good education."

Finally, the banker said, "Mrs. Morton and I would be able to give the boy a fine home and a fine education. We would like him to come and live with us."

The presiding officer looked around and asked, "Is there anyone else who would like to say anything?" From the back row, a man rose and said, "These other people may be able to offer some things I can't. All I can offer is my love." Then, he slowly removed his hands from his coat pockets. A gasp went up from the crowd because his hands were scarred terribly from climbing up and down the hot pipe. The boy recognized the man as the one who had saved his life and ran into his waiting arms.

The farmer, teacher and the banker simply sat down. Everyone knew what the decision would be. The scarred hands proved that this man was interested in the boy. The scarred hands spoke of his love for the boy.

Today, there are many things which are vying for our love and attention. Young and old alike are challenged by the call of money, pleasure, fame and a host of other interests. But let us never forget that down the corridors of time walks one who, by merely raising his hands, reminds us of his claim upon us. Those hands were pierced by nails. Those hands were a sign of recognition to the disciples. Those hands are a reminder that there is one who loves us.

III. The Hands Of Jesus Remind Us That We Are Called To Act On Our Faith.

Thomas had doubts about the resurrection when he heard the stories of the disciples. His doubts were clear and he said to the disciples, "Unless I see his hands myself . . . I will not believe." Thomas was full of doubts and had his mind closed to everything until he was confronted with the risen Christ. Jesus looked at Thomas and said, "Thomas, if it's proof that you want, look at my hands, touch the wounds and stop your doubting."

Thomas looked at the hands and knew that action was needed. Instead of touching the wounds, Thomas fell to the ground and said, "My Lord and my God."

Sometimes, you have to discard your doubts and act on faith. You may have some lingering doubts. You may have some unanswered questions. You may have some things which will remain a mystery. But, like Thomas, we sometimes reach that point where we need to translate our doubts into acts of faith.

Several years ago, my wife made me a little banner. It was a short little phrase that I like. Whenever I am facing a difficult situation or wondering which way I should go, I look up from my desk and read the words on that banner: "Faith is walking to the edge of all the light you have and taking one more step."

Faith is coming to that point where we are standing on the edge of doubt and we can see no clear path ahead, but we go on in faith. We go on in spite of doubts. We go on in the faith that God is with us.

When the history of this century is written, there will be the names of many prominent men and women. However, there is one name that I believe will be forever remembered — and that is Winston Churchill.

Hitler had conquered Europe and was on the verge of conquering England. Churchill had doubts that England would be able to survive, but he could not permit his doubts to show. His task was to rally the British Empire and help the British people to act to save themselves. With a marvelous ability to lead and inspire people with his words, Churchill helped to translate the doubts of the British people into acts of faith. On one occasion, Churchill said:

> *"When I look back on the perils which we have already overcome, and upon the great mountain waves through which the ship has been driven, when I remember all that has gone right, I am encouraged to feel we need not be afraid that the tempest will overcome us. Let it roar. Let it rage. We shall come through."*

I think the Lord must have loved Winston Churchill. He translated his doubts into actions of faith. He helped his people see beyond the doubts in their minds and begin acting on the faith and hope of overcoming the storm.

Doubts are a reality in our lives. We all have occasional doubts. We all have questions which need answers. We would all like to have absolute proof. But, sometimes, we need to respond as Thomas did. We need to look at the hands of Jesus Christ and act on our faith by falling on our knees and saying as he did: "My Lord and my God."

Are you ready to act on your faith? Are you ready to take one more step into the unknown future with faith in Jesus Christ?

Prayer: O God, in these moments, lead us to open our hearts, our lives and our souls to the risen Christ. In his name. Amen.

The Third Sunday Of Easter
Luke 24:13-35

Encounter With A Stranger

I had just sat down to eat with a group in the fellowship hall. There was a covered-dish dinner and everyone had brought their favorite recipes. The food looked delicious and the desserts looked even better. Just as I was about to take my first bite, someone told me there was a man in the hallway who would like to speak to the pastor.

I slipped out of the fellowsihp hall to find this man who wanted to see me. When I rounded the corner, I saw him standing down at the end of the hall. One glance and I knew that he was one of the homeless we see so often roaming the streets. He spotted me and began walking down the hallway toward me. There was a weariness in every step he took. His face had the leathery look of a man who was familiar with all kinds of weather. His clothes were ragged and he had the look of a man who had had to make do for a very long time.

I greeted him and asked what I could do for him. He told me he was hungry and wanted to know if I could help him get something to eat. I invited him in to eat with our group. He was hesitant to join our group, so I offered to get him a plate of food. I took him to another room and let him sit down to eat.

As he was eating, I asked, "How long have you been on the road?"

"A long time," he said, "a very long time."

"Where do you live?" I asked.

"I travel a lot," he said. "Most nights the stars are my roof and the earth is my bed."

"Haven't you ever thought of settling down and having a home?"

"I tried it once," he said, "but it didn't work out. I just wasn't happy settled in one place."

"What do you call yourself?" I asked the hungry man.

"My name is Joshua," he said.

"Did you know that is a name from the Bible?" I asked. "Joshua means 'God's salvation.' "

He looked at me with a surprised look on his face and he smiled. He thanked me for the hot meal and buttoned his coat and headed for the door. When he was gone, I remembered that story from the Bible about Cleopas and his companion and their encounter with a stranger on the road to Emmaus. This story, as recorded in the Gospel of Luke, is one of the great short stories in all of literature. It tells of two men walking along the Emmaus Road. The waves of heat shimmered above the dusty road as they put Jerusalem farther and farther behind them.

As they walked along, they spoke of the events which had taken place in the Holy City. So much had happened in just a few days. In fact, everything happened so quickly that it all seemed like a terrible dream. There had been Christ's triumphant entry into the Holy City. Then, the joy of that moment gave way to fear as a net of intrigue was woven around the Nazarene. The agony of the crucifixion at Calvary still haunted them. They had seen the dead, limp body of Jesus removed from the cross and laid in the borrowed tomb of Joseph of Arimathea. And yet, there were now whisperings and rumors spreading throughout Jerusalem that Jesus was alive.

These were the things that Cleopas and his companion talked about on the road to Emmaus. The more they talked, the more engrossed they became. They were so engrossed in their own conversation, that they did not notice the approach of a stranger. Suddenly, there he was walking with them.

The stranger asks, "What are you talking about to each other as you walk along?"

Cleopas and his companion are amazed at the question and they answer by saying, "You must be the only visitor in Jerusalem who does not know the things that have happened there recently."

And the stranger asks, "What things?"

And they begin to relate the sad events about Jesus which this stranger had apparently not heard. The stranger listens and then shares his own beliefs about Jesus. He began with Moses and all the prophets and explained to these two men on the Emmaus Road all the scripture that referred to Jesus.

The conversation made the seven-and-one-half mile walk pass quickly. When they reached the city of Emmaus, the sun was sinking fast in the western sky, darkness was approaching and they invited the stranger to spend the night.

As they sat down to eat the evening meal, Cleopas asks the stranger to give the blessing for the meal. There was something in the way he gave thanks. There was something in the way he took the bread and broke it. There was something about his gestures that were recognizable. Perhaps, the folds of his robe fell back and they saw the livid red marks of the nails in his hands. But, whatever it was, in that instant they knew him. In that moment they recognized him. In that fraction of a second they knew that their encounter with a stranger had been an encounter with the risen Lord. And he was gone! It wasn't possible! It couldn't be, but they had seen him with their own eyes and heard him with their own ears. They got up and ran the seven-and-one-half miles back to Jerusalem to tell the other disciples the incredible news of their encounter with a stranger.

Today, as we look at this story of the encounter with the stranger along the road to Emmaus, there are three things which I think are important.

I. The Encounter With The Stranger Shed Light On That Which Was Confusing.

There is an old story of a young preacher who went to chapel services one day at seminary. He heard one of the professors say in his sermon, "The happiest days of my life were spent in the arms of another man's wife — my mother."

The young preacher thought the quotation would add drama and force to his sermon the next Sunday, so he tried it. He said, "The happiest days of my life were spent in the arms of another man's wife." At this point he had a mental block. He was confused. He was bewildered. He agonized for a moment and then he said, "The happiest days of my life were spent in the arms of another man's wife — but I can't remember who it was to save my life."

Just as that young preacher was confused; so were the two men walking along the Emmaus Road. The events that had taken place in Jerusalem left them confused. Their hopes and dreams had been shattered. You can catch the confusion and regret in their voices when they looked at the stranger and told him all the recent events concerning Jesus of Nazareth. There was a note of sorrow and confusion in their voices as they said: "And we had hoped that he would be the one who was going to set Israel free!"

These are the words of men whose hopes are dead, whose dreams are buried and whose minds are confused.

And then Jesus began to talk to them and explain the meaning of everything that had taken place. He began with Moses and all the prophets and tried to shed some light on their confusion. As he talked with them, they gradually began to understand. The meaning came clear to them. The darkness was replaced with the dawning of light. They began to understand there was someone walking with them and helping them to understand.

A couple of years ago, a television anchorwoman in New York City, named Pat Harper, wanted to understand the plight of the homeless. She left her luxurious East Side apartment with 80 cents in her pocket. She spent five days living on the street to learn what it was like to be homeless. She spent her days wandering the streets in the icy January rain. She spent her nights sleeping in doorways, train stations and public shelters. She ate in soup kitchens and street missions.

The undercover investigation made her realize that many homeless people are simply normal people who have been hit with serious financial problems. These people helped her, gave her advice on how to survive without money and even shared what little food they had. There was no other way for this successful television anchorwoman to understand the homeless than to walk where they walked.

This was the message that was made clear to these two men on the Emmaus Road. Their encounter with the stranger shed light on their confusion and helped them to understand that Jesus Christ was walking with them.

II. The Encounter With The Stranger Brings A Recognition Of Love And A Sense Of Joy.

Why didn't Cleopas and his companion recognize Jesus when he first approached them on the Emmaus Road? No one knows! The Bible simply says, "They saw him, but somehow did not recognize him . . ."

Perhaps, they had seen him crucified on a cross and they simply didn't expect to see him again. Whatever the reason, they walked along the dusty road and listened to this stranger. When they reached Emmaus, they invited this stranger to share their evening meal and spend the night in their home.

It was here in their home that they recognized him. Was it the way he broke the loaf of bread? Was it a familiar gesture? Was it a glimpse of a hand which had known the print of a nail? Whatever it was, a silence falls over the table. No one moves. No one speaks. They just know. There is a recognition of love. And, there is joy at that recognition.

David Redding tells of having a big, black Scottish shepherd as a pet when he was growing up on a farm in the country. He named the dog Teddy and they became inseparable companions. Teddy would wait on him to come home from school at the bus stop. Teddy slept at the foot of his bed. Teddy came whenever David whistled a tune. During the night, no one could get within a half mile of their farm without Teddy's permission. The boy and his dog were inseparable.

Then World War II came and David went away to war. He told his family good-bye, but there was no way to tell a dog you were going away and might never come back.

David Redding went away to boot camp and then was shipped overseas for three years. Finally, the day came when he could go home. The last bus stop was 14 miles from the farm and his parents didn't have a phone. He simply threw his duffle bag over his shoulder and started walking. It must have been two o'clock in the morning as he neared the farm. It was pitch dark, but he knew every step of the way. Suddenly, the dog heard someone on the road and began to bark. David said, "I whistled only once and Teddy stopped barking. There was a yelp of recognition, and I knew that a big, black dog was running toward me in the darkness. Almost immediately, he was there and in my arms. He knew me. He recognized me. He loved me. Even after three years, he recognized me and loved me."

Whenever there is a recognition of love, there is joy. Cleopas and his companion made a marvelous discovery that evening in their home. They recognized the risen Lord. They recognized that he was with them. And this recognition brought joy to their lives.

I cannot make many promises to you. But, there is one promise of which I am absolutely positive. When you reach that point where you recognize God's love in Jesus Christ, you will be filled with an inner sense of happiness and peace.

III. The Encounter With The Stranger Reminds Us That When We Experience Joy, We Want To Share It.

When Cleopas and his companion recognized the risen Christ, they experienced a joy they wanted to share. They said to each other, "Wasn't it like a fire burning in us?" It was such an exciting experience of joy that they wanted to share. So, they got up and headed back toward Jerusalem. It was seven-and-one-half miles to Jerusalem. It was dark and the road could be treacherous at night, but they had incredible news and they wanted to share it with others.

A few years ago, Madalyne and I went to the OU-Texas ball game in Dallas. Our seats were right in the end zone and the OU Sooners were scoring a bunch of touchdowns. Every time they scored and got ready to kick an extra point, I noticed a man with a multi-colored wig — striped in red, blue, green and orange. He would position himself so the television cameras would have to pick him up when they showed the extra point attempt. He would hold up a sign that in bold letters said:

John 3:16
Romans 5:8
Galatians 4:4

I recognized the man because he is seen on television all the time at nationally televised football games, the World Series and golf tournaments.

During halftime, I went and stood in line at the concession stand. The man with the multi-colored wig was standing in front of me and we got to talking. I asked him what got him started going to all those ballgames and holding up signs with scripture passages.

He said, "There was a time in my life when I was addicted to alcohol and drugs. They had me by the throat and they were choking the life out of me. My life was falling apart. Someone gave me a Bible and I started reading it. I discovered Jesus Christ and let him take control of my life. I go to all of these ball games and hold up the signs because I want to get people to read the book and discover the joy I discovered in Jesus Christ!"

That man in the multi-colored wig may not be sharing the good news the same way that you or I would, but you have to admire his determination. How are you sharing your experience of joy with Jesus Christ? Remember, the joy of faith in Jesus is never really ours until we hasten to share it with others.

How are you sharing your faith in Christ?

Prayer: O God, give to us the courage to share our faith with others. In the name of Jesus Christ, Amen.

The Fourth Sunday Of Easter
John 21:1-14

Breakfast In Galilee

I do not usually eat a big breakfast. Most of the time I just have a bowl of cereal, a piece of toast and a glass of juice. A couple of weeks ago, on a Sunday morning, we were out of milk, so I just headed off toward the church. On the way, I decided to go to a restaurant, grab a bite to eat and look over my sermon notes before church services.

When the waitress came to take my order, I ordered the cereal, toast and juice. The waitress smiled and said, "Dr. Allen, that puny little breakfast won't get you through today's services."

I looked up at this waitress, smiled, and asked, "What would you recommend?"

"Oh," she said, "you need something that will stick with you all morning. I would suggest some scrambled eggs, hash browns and biscuits and gravy."

"That sounds pretty good," I said. "I think I'll try your suggestion."

She smiled and started to walk away and I asked, "Do we know each other?"

"Oh no," she said, "we've never met. Since I work on Sundays, I don't get a chance to go to church very much. So, sometimes I watch your service on television."

"What do you like about our services?" I asked.

She said, "I like the fact that you remind people that, regardless of what they have done, they are still loved by God."

And this is the message that John's gospel is proclaiming in the story of Jesus fixing breakfast for the disciples along the shore of the Sea of Galilee. Now, to be honest, many scholars question whether this chapter was added at a later date. Many scholars say this chapter was an appendix to the gospel.

Regardless of when this chapter was written, it is a story vividly told of the disciples spending the night fishing. They had worked hard all night and had caught nothing. As they rowed the boat back toward the shore, they were tired, they were hungry and they were discouraged. After all, they had seen the risen Lord. They had been given some bold and audacious promises by him. They had been called to a high service for him and the world. And yet, day after day crept by and nothing had happened. As they rowed toward shore on this calm morning, they were discouraged and silent. Each person seemed to be lost in their own thoughts as someone standing on the shore called out: ". . . have you caught anything?" And when they replied in the negative, the person on shore called out: "Throw your nets on the right side and you will catch some."

When they followed this advice, they caught so many fish they could barely haul them into the boat. It was at this time that they recognized it was the Lord. Impulsively, Peter jumped in the water and waded ashore. The others brought the boat ashore and Jesus invited them to a breakfast along the shore of Galilee by saying, "Come and dine."

Apparently, Jesus had prepared this meal with his own hands. He had used hot coals to build a good fire. He had baked some bread. He used some of the fish they caught and Jesus cooked a breakfast for these tired and hungry disciples that fed their bodies and nourished their souls.

Now, why is this story about Jesus cooking breakfast in Galilee here? There are, of course, many reasons suggested.

Today, I want us to look at and examine some of the reasons that Jesus had breakfast in Galilee with the disciples.

I. Jesus Had Breakfast In Galilee To Remind The Disciples That He Was Who He Said He Was.

After Hubert Humphrey lost the presidential campaign of 1968, he returned to his home state of Minnesota. He took a job teaching at a university and began making plans to regain his seat in the U.S Senate.

One of his longtime friends and advisers was Judge Miles Lord. They went on a fishing trip in northern Minnesota and stopped at a sporting goods store in a small town to buy some supplies. While in the store, Judge Lord noticed a tour bus from California had broken down outside.

The judge decided to play a practical joke and sneaked out to the bus and introduced himself as the mayor of the town. He said to the people on the bus: "Folks, I'm sorry you're having trouble in our town. If there's anything we can do for you, just stop by my office. And by the way, there's something you can do for us. We have a fellow here in town who looks like our former vice president, Hubert Humphrey. He sounds like Hubert Humphrey. He even thinks he is Hubert Humphrey. Now, you probably won't even run into him. But, if you do, don't give him any money. Just be nice to him and humor him. He doesn't do any harm."

The judge excused himself and went back into the store. He said, "Hubert, there's a bus load of California tourists out in the parking lot dying to meet you."

Of course, Humphrey went out and climbed on the bus and began shaking hands. When he went back in the store, the judge asked him how it went. "You know," Humphrey said, "those California people are kind of strange. Every time I shook hands with one of them and told them I was Hubert Humphrey, someone would start to giggle."

Mistaken identities can make people laugh and giggle. Although the disciples had encountered the risen Christ, they probably had to face the ridicules, the scorn and even the jeers of the other people of Israel.

They had seen the risen Lord and their hopes were high for the future. But, then he was gone and they were left to sit idly around. They were left to sit around and wait. They were left to sit around and wonder if they had been dreaming. They were left to sit around and wonder if Jesus really was who he said he was.

Into such a moment of doubt and discouragement, Jesus came and fixed them breakfast along the shores of Galilee. Jesus came to remind them that the resurrection was not some romantic wish which had taken control of their imagination. Jesus came to remind them that he was who he said he was — the resurrected Messiah.

II. Jesus Had Breakfast In Galilee To Remind The Disciples That Their Mission Was To Salvage Souls.

Years ago, when I was in school, I took a class in archaeology. One of the things that we had to do in that class was go with the professor to one of his digs along the Brazos River. The site was the location of an ancient Indian village. The village was abandoned hundreds of years ago, but lying buried there under many layers of dirt was the evidence of the ancient civilization. With careful digging and sifting of the dirt, the professor and the other archaeologist involved in the project were salvaging ancient pieces of pottery. They were salvaging ancient artifacts. They were salvaging bits and pieces of an ancient civilization.

Such attempts at salvaging have added significantly to the wealth of the world. The treasures found in ancient ships, lost at sea, make the finder rich. The treasures found in ancient pyramids, buried by the sands of time, tell us of long forgotten kingdoms. The treasures found in ancient cities, abandoned or destroyed, tell us how people long ago lived. The finding of these treasures capture our imagination.

However, there is another kind of salvaging which is more important than digging up the relics of the past. And that is the salvaging of human souls. This is important because each person — each soul — is more precious in the sight of God than all the silver and gold in this world.

The salvaging of human souls was Jesus' mission in our world. Throughout his ministry, he said over and over again: "The Son of Man is come to seek and to save that which was lost." As he traveled up and down the dusty roads of Palestine, the salvaging of souls was the driving force behind every sermon he preached, behind every miracle he performed, behind every personal encounter he had and even the ultimate explanation, behind his willingness to face the cross of Calgary.

Because our Lord gave himself so completely to the work of salvaging souls, is it any wonder that here, just before his ascension, he would come to be with his disciples? Is it any wonder that he would come to share a meal with them? Is it any wonder that he would come to remind them that their mission was to continue the work of salvaging souls by proclaiming the good news? Is it any wonder that he would come to remind them that their mission was to turn the world upside down proclaiming God's love for everyone?

And this is our challenge if we are to be his disciples in today's world. We are to proclaim the good news of God's love in Jesus Christ. We are to take seriously the work of salvaging souls. We are called to turn our world upside down by proclaiming God's love through the living of our faith.

Out of all the stories I've ever told, my favorite is one told by J. Wallace Hamilton in his book *What About Tomorrow?* It is a story about a Baptist minister, Dr. Gordon Torgerson, sailing across the Atlantic one summer. He noticed a dark skinned man sitting in a deck chair reading the Bible. He sat down beside him and said, "Forgive my curiosity, but I'm a Baptist minister. I assume you are a Christian, and I'm interested to know how it happened."

"Yes," said the dark skinned man, setting aside his Bible. "I'm very glad to talk about that. I'm a Filipino. I was born in a good Catholic home in the Philippines. Some years ago, I came to the United States to study law. My first night on campus, a student came to see me. He said, 'I've come to welcome you to the campus and to say that if there is anything I can do to help make your stay here more pleasant, I hope you'll call on me.' Then he asked me where I went to church and I told him I was a Catholic. He said, 'Well, I can tell you where the Catholic church is, but it's not easy to find. It's quite a distance away. Let me make a map.' So he made an outline of the way to the church and left.

"When I awakened Sunday morning, it was raining. I thought to myself, I'll just not go to church today. I'll get some more sleep.

"Then there was a knock on the door and when I opened it there stood that student. His raincoat was dripping wet and on one arm he had two umbrellas, and he said, 'I thought you might have a hard time finding your church in the rain. I shall walk along with you and show you the way.'

"As we walked along in the rain under the two umbrellas I asked, 'Where do you go to church?'

" 'Oh,' he said, 'my church is just around the corner.'

"I said, 'Suppose we go to your church today and we'll go to my church next Sunday.'

"I went to his church and I've never been back to my own. After four years, I felt it was not the law for me, but the ministry. I went to Drew Seminary and was ordained a Methodist minister, and received an appointment to a Methodist church in the Philippines. My name is Valencius. I am Bishop Valencius, Bishop of the Methodist Church in the Philippines."

That is a fascinating story of one of the most important people in the world — not the bishop, though he is important — but the man with the two umbrellas. In back of every convert to the Christian faith, in back of every church that was built, in back of every Christian enterprise and movement in history, you will find someone like that unnamed fellow with two umbrellas. An ordinary man or woman, a person who believed that the salvaging of souls was important, a person who dared to make his faith so useful, a person who dared to make her faith so attractive, that other people said, "I want the kind of faith you have!"

We can turn the world upside down when we dare to live out our faith because we believe that each person is precious to God.

Will you dare to do that?

Will you dare to be the person with two umbrellas?

Will you dare to make your faith so attractive that others will be willing to walk with you to the foot of the cross?

Prayer: O God, may your love shine in us and through us so that others may come to know your Son, Jesus Christ. In his name. Amen.

The Fifth Sunday Of Easter
John 21:15-19

Do You Love Me?

There is a very tender and moving scene in the play, *Fiddler On The Roof*. Tevyev and his wife Golda are being forced to move from their home in Russia. One day Tevyev comes into the house and asks his wife, "Golda, do you love me?"

"Do I what?"

"Do you love me?"

Golda looks at him and then responds: "Do I love you? With our daughters getting married and this trouble in the town, you're upset, you're worn out, go inside, go lie down, maybe it's indigestion."

Tevyev interrupts and asks the question, "Golda, do you love me?"

Golda sighs as she looked at him and says, "Do I love you? For 25 years I've washed your clothes, cooked your meals, cleaned your house, given you children, milked the cows. After 25 years, why talk of love right now?"

Tevyev answers by saying, "Golda, the first time I met you was on our wedding day. I was scared, I was shy, I was nervous."

"So was I," said Golda.

"But my father and my mother said we'd learn to love each other, and now I'm asking, "Golda, do you love me?"

"Do I love him?" Golda sighs. "For 25 years I've lived with him, fought with him, 25 years my bed is his! If that's not love, what is?"

"Then you love me?" Tevyev asks.

"I suppose I do!" she says.

"And I suppose I love you too!" he says. "It doesn't change a thing, but after 25 years it's nice to know."

"Do you love me?" is the same question Jesus is asking Peter in the closing scene of the Gospel of John. It is interesting to note that this closing scene is cast in the same spot where the first scenes of the gospel took place — on the shore of the Sea of Galilee. Once again Peter was back to his old occupation. Once again Peter was back to his old way of life. Once again Peter was back in his old fishing boat. But it was not a very exciting return. Peter and the other disciples had spent the entire night fishing, but they had caught nothing.

Throughout that long and frustrating night of fishing, the thoughts of Peter keep flying back to another occasion, another time. He was remembering how one had stood on the shore almost three years ago and said to him: "Come, follow me and I will make you a fisher of men."

Dreams of those happy days were dancing in his mind. Suddenly, John was shaking him and pointing toward the shore. Peter looked toward the shore and saw someone and asked, "Who is it?"

"Can't you see?" cried John. "It's the Lord!"

Again, Peter looked toward the shore. He recognized Jesus. He leaped into the water. He went to meet Jesus. Later, when Peter and Jesus are alone, Jesus asks a question that goes to the heart of Peter. He asks: "Simon, son of Jonas, do you love me more than these?"

Three times Jesus asks this question: "Simon, do you love me?"

And three times Peter responds by saying: "Yes, Lord, you know I love you."

And three times Jesus commissioned Peter: "Feed my sheep!"

Many preachers and scholars, when they get to this point in the biblical story, want to focus on the three questions that Jesus asked, or the three responses of Peter or the challenge of Jesus to "feed my sheep." Instead of going in that direction, I want to look at the loving way in which Jesus dealt with Peter. Love is something we talk about. Love is something we romanticize about. Love is something we know we need more of. However, by watching Jesus deal with Peter along the shore of the Sea of Galilee, we get a good clear picture of love in action.

I. One Thing Which We See In The Example Of Jesus Is That Love Is Caring.

As Peter found himself alone with Jesus by the Sea of Galilee, I would imagine there was an awkward silence. After all, Peter was probably feeling guilty about denying Jesus when he was warming himself by the fire at Caiaphas' house. Peter was probably trying to figure out how to put the apology into words. But Jesus deals with the awkward situation by asking a very simple question. He looks at Peter and asks: "Simon do you love me?"

Jesus could have handled that awkward situation in a very judgmental way. He could have asked, "Simon, are you ashamed of denying me?" He could have said, "Simon, I understand you lied about knowing me." He could have asked, "Simon, how can I be sure you won't deny me in the future?" But Jesus knew how Peter was hurting in his heart, so he went right to the heart of the matter by asking: "Simon, do you love me?" By asking this question three times, perhaps this was Jesus' way of helping Peter overcome his earlier denials.

However, one thing is clear and that is that Jesus dealt very carefully with Peter. Jesus did not attempt to further embarrass Peter or to compound his guilt. Instead, he asked a simple little question, a question that was direct, but a question that was tempered with a love that was caring and compassionate.

A few years ago I was in Washington, D.C., and I went on a tour of all the traditional sites like the White House, the Smithsonian, the halls of Congress and the Lincoln Memorial. There is something about standing in the Lincoln Memorial and reading the Gettysburg Address and the Second Inaugural Address which gives you goosebumps. One line in the Second Inaugural reminds you what a caring and compassionate man Lincoln was. He was speaking about the coming end of the War and he said: "With malice toward none; With charity for all."

Lincoln put this idea into practice on the day that news arrived in Washington that the war was over. A crowd gathered at the White House and a military band was playing some festive music. Lincoln stood on the balcony of the White House and spoke. Instead of lashing out against the South, he spoke of the horrors of war being over. He spoke of families getting back together. He spoke of a time of peace. Then he said, "In a few moments I want the band to play and I'm going to tell them what I want them to play."

Of course, the band started getting the "Battle Hymn of The Republic" ready to play. This had been the theme song of the North throughout the Civil War. But Lincoln crossed them up. He stood there and said: "The band will now play the theme song of the people we have called our enemy. They are not our enemies any more! We are one people again. I want the band to play 'Dixie.' "

Historians say there was a long, awkward pause. The band didn't have the music to "Dixie," but they finally got together and played, "Dixie." Lincoln knew that the South was not only hurting because of the horrors of the war, but also because of the shame which accompanies defeat. Lincoln was sending a clear signal to the South. Lincoln was telling everyone that there would be no punishment upon the South. Lincoln was saying that the South would be treated with love and compassion.

When you love, after the patterns of Jesus, caring and compassion become the cornerstone of your love. Love is not vicious or hostile. Love does not try to compound the guilt. Love doesn't try to rub salt in the wounds of shame.

When we learn to love after the pattern of Jesus, we learn to show care. We learn to show understanding. We learn to show compassion to those who are hurting.

II. A Second Thing We See In The Example Of Jesus Is That Love Is Forgiving.

Peter must have been hurting on the inside. After all, look what he had done. He had denied even knowing Jesus. He had shamed himself by cursing those who accused him of being a disciple. He had used language so vile that even the soldiers were shocked. And now, alone with Jesus by the Sea of Galilee, Peter was looking for a way to prove his love for Jesus. But what could he do? He could not appeal to his record of faithfulness because his record was smeared with shame. He could not appeal to his reputation as a man of his word, for that reputation evaporated the night he denied knowing Jesus on three occasions. He could not appeal to the witness and testimony of his fellow disciples because they knew that when the chips were down, fear turned Peter into a coward. Peter had nothing, absolutely nothing, to prove his love was genuine.

But, was Peter really left with nothing? Three times Jesus asked, "Simon, do you love me?" And three times Peter responded: "Lord, you know all things. You know the whole story. You know everything about me. You know I love you."

Peter had nothing left with which to prove his love. And yet, Peter sensed deep within that he did not have to prove his love. He knew that he did not have to prove his loyalty. He knew that the heart of Jesus would be forgiving for his shortcomings.

This is the way the love of Jesus is — it is forgiving. Forgiveness did not take away Peter's memory of his denial — he carried that memory with him to his grave. The forgiveness of Jesus simply re-established the old relationship and assured Peter he was still loved. This is the way of Jesus' love — it is forgiving. In spite of the sin in our lives, in spite of the wrong we do, in spite of the guilt and shame we bring on ourselves, the love of Jesus is a love that is forgiving.

In a novel, a woman is in the hospital with a terminal illness. Her life has been lived on the wild side. Her life has been as bad and as despicable as they come. Now, she is dying.

A priest, a friend for many years, is in the room with her and she asks, "Am I dying?"

"Yes," the priest said.

"Does he love me?" the woman asked.

"Your husband?" the priest asked.

"No," she said. "You know who I'm talking about. Does God love me?"

The priest said, "Yes, God loves you!"

"I find that hard to believe," the woman said. "You know the kind of life I've lived. How can you say that God still loves me?"

The priest smiled at her question and said, "I'm telling you that no matter what you've done, God still loves you." Then the priest began reading one of the beautiful prayers in the Last Rites of the Catholic Church. He read the prayer which says: "God loves you and God accepts you. Your sins are forgiven; you belong to God; You are now with God."

This is the message which came through to Peter along the shores of the Sea of Galilee. And it is the message which we need to hear. In spite of our sins, in spite of our failures, in spite of everything we have ever done which denies him, his love forgives us and accepts us because we belong to him.

Are you ready to accept his forgiving love?

Are you ready to once again try to be one of his followers?

Prayer: O God, help us to know that your love forgives us and claims us as your disciples. In Jesus' name. Amen.

The Sixth Sunday Of Easter
Matthew 28:16-20

One More Thing

When I was a kid growing up, I don't think I ever went anywhere without my mother saying, "Robert, there is one more thing I want to tell you." It didn't make any difference where I was going. I could have been going to camp, I could have been going to spend the night with a friend or I could have been going to a party. I don't care what it was, before I got out of the car, my mother would say, "There's one more thing I want to tell you."

It was never really one more thing — but several things. And they were usually always the same. My mother would look at me and she would say, "Remember, be on your best manners. Don't do anything to embarrass the family." Another thing she always asked was a question I hated. But, I'll bet many of your mothers asked you the same thing. She would get a serious look on her face and ask, "Robert, are you wearing your good underwear? If anything serious ever happened, I'd hate for anyone to see your holey underwear."

Do you know the thought that always went through my mind? I could imagine an accident and I would be rushed to the emergency room and the doctor working on me would say, "Look at these holes in his underwear. Get his mother in here right away. I want to talk to her."

One more thing which my mother would say before I got out of the car. She would look at me, her eyes would soften and she would say, "Remember, I love you."

I suppose that I will always remember my mother's concern for me and her way of saying, "There's one more thing I want to tell you."

When we look at the scripture for today, the gospel of Matthew is coming to a close and Jesus has one more thing he wants to tell his disciples. The parting words of Jesus have done more to emphasize his teaching. The parting words of Jesus have done more to give us a vision of a world-wide church. The parting words of Jesus have done more to send disciples into all nations with the good news of God's love in Jesus Christ. The parting words of Jesus have done more than any other part of the Bible in presenting the magnificent theme of God's salvation available for all people.

Whenever we read this particular scripture, we have a tendency to see only the Great Commission which says, "Go ye therefore and make disciples of all nations, baptizing them in the name of the Father, and of the Son, and of the Holy Spirit." However, when we look closely and listen carefully, the last words of Jesus to his disciples really did three things. There is a claim of power. There is a great commission. There is the promise of a presence. The one more thing which Jesus had to say to his disciples was a summation of his teachings.

Today, as we look at the parting words of Jesus to his disciples and to the whole church, I want us to look at all three things.

I. Jesus Assured Us Of His Power

When you read Matthew 28:18 in different translations, you will notice that one key word is different. Most translations have Jesus say, "All authority in heaven and on earth has been given to me." I don't believe those translations which use the word "authority" really capture the true meaning of

Jesus. In this particular passage, I believe that the King James version is more accurate when it translates that verse. The King James version says: "All power is given unto me in heaven and in earth."

Now, I realize that you did not come to church today hoping I would conjugate Greek words for you. I simply want to say that the word "authority" means the right to appoint to an office while the word "power" is the claim to a purpose. Jesus was claiming the power to accomplish a purpose. Power is not power unless it can accomplish the purpose to which it is applied. A chain saw is great for cutting fine wood, but it can't be used by a man to shave his beard in the morning. Dynamite is a powerful device for blowing away part of a mountain, but for the purpose of blowing out candles on a birthday cake, it is not very effective.

Atomic bombs and nuclear-tipped missiles are great for destroying life as we know it on this planet, but if the purpose is to cleanse our hearts of hate and to help people to find their way to peace with God and with each other, then the atomic bomb is not the kind of power that is needed.

The power that is needed is the power to accomplish a purpose. This is the kind of power that Jesus claims. He does not claim a power of coercion, but the power of persuasion. He does not claim a power of force, but a power of devotion from within. He does not claim a dictatorial power, but the power where people can freely choose.

In a courtroom one day in Jerusalem, Pilate, representing the kingdom and force of the Roman empire looked at Jesus and asked, "Don't you know that I have the power?" Jesus, standing before Pilate with his hands tied behind his back, and the spittle of a Roman soldier on his face said, "My kingdom ... my power ... is not of this world."

Think about the difference there in Pilate's hall. We are a people who have been obsessed with Pilate's kind of power. But Pilate, Caesar, Alexander, Napoleon and Stalin founded their empires upon the power of force and they are all gone. Jesus Christ used another kind of power — the power of love — and his kingdom has grown from a small group of disciples to literally millions and millions of men and women who have freely chosen to follow him.

The reality of his power in this is clearly shown in the words of a little poem which says:

Nineteen centuries have come and gone
And today he is the central figure of the human race,
All of the armies that ever marched,
All of the navies that ever sailed,
All of the parliaments that ever sat,
And all of the kings that ever reigned,
Have not affected the life of man on this earth
as much as that one solitary life — (Jesus Christ)

If we want God's power in our hands, we must have his kind of power in our hearts — power to accomplish his purpose.

II. Jesus Gave Us A Commission

Jesus sent his disciples out into the world with the commission to win men and women to faith in him. This commission was not just for those first disciples, but is for all disciples — including you and me.

I know a man who had been successful in life. And then, everything started to go wrong. He lost his business. He lost his money. He lost everything he had worked for in life. One day, in the midst of his discouragement and despair, he tried to commit suicide. But, he failed! While he was in the hospital recovering, one of his friends came in the room and simply asked, "Why did you do it, Joe? Why did you do it?"

Joe looked over at him and said, "Because there isn't any good news left in the world. If there was, someone would have told me."

This is what the great commission is about — one person telling another the good news. Jesus expected his disciples to go throughout the world with the good news that would transform the world, change the world and convert the world. And he expected the same of us as his modern day disciples. But, we have become so comfortable at sitting in our pews that we no longer are going out into the world and telling the good news.

I preached in a little church in Southwestern Oklahoma one Sunday evening. It was a little white-framed Methodist church with a cemetery out behind the church. There was a center aisle and two side aisles. When you entered the church, if someone forgot to tie the rope to the bell tower out of the way, you could walk right into it. It was a typical country church.

What I liked about this country church were the words which were painted in golf-leaf over the door. As you were leaving the church, these words were posted over the door so you would see them. The words were: "You Are Entering The Mission Field."

Isn't that why Jesus commissioned us as his disciples? We gather in this sanctuary to worship. We gather in this sanctuary to grow in our faith. We gather in this sanctuary for fellowship with one another. We gather in this sanctuary to sense our oneness in Jesus Christ. Then, we go out into the mission field — the world where we live and work and play. It is in the mission field of our world where we are to proclaim the good news. It is in the mission field of our world where we are sent to set at liberty those who are oppressed. It is in the mission field of our world where we are to proclaim this to be the time to take up your cross and follow Jesus Christ.

We have a commission from Jesus. Our commission is to be his witness and make disciples in his name! Will you be obedient to his commission?

III. Jesus Promised Us A Presence

It must have been a staggering thing for 11 disciples to be sent forth to conquer the world for a risen Savior. There must have been doubts and fears in their minds as they contemplated how they would carry out their commission. But, no sooner was the command given than the promise followed. They were sent out — as we are — on the greatest task in the world. But, there was also the promise that they would not be alone. The promise of Jesus was "Lo, I am with you always, even unto the end of the world."

Almost 20 years ago, the attention of the world was focused on three men who were close to a quarter of a million miles away from the earth. The Apollo 13 spacecraft was making a trip to the moon. Somewhere, out there in the darkness of space, there was an explosion aboard their spacecraft. They lost power. They were not generating oxygen. They didn't know if they would have the fuel to return to the planet earth.

Everyone held their breath and said their prayers, as the NASA scientists and engineers tried to figure out a way to bring these astronauts home. In order to conserve oxygen, the astronauts were ordered to crawl into the lunar lander and remain in there for the three-day trip back toward home.

These men were not sure if they would make it home. They didn't know if their oxygen would hold out. They didn't know if their thrusters would fire for re-entry into the earth's atmosphere. They didn't know if they would skip off the earth's atmosphere like a rock skipping across the pond and wander for eternity through the darkness of space.

But, they did make it home. After their splash down in the ocean, they were taken aboard an aircraft carrier for medical exams. As they were sitting in the examining room, one of the astronauts looked at the other two and said, "I don't know if you felt the same thing I did or not. But, when we were cramped in that lunar lander wondering if we would make it home, I felt as though we were not alone. I don't know how to put it into words, but I felt the presence of God was there with us."

The promise of Jesus is a promise that we will never be alone. He said to his disciples and he said to each of us, "Lo, I am with you always, even unto the end of the world."

Can you sense God's presence with you now? Where is God? Here within! A poem says it so simply:

As near as green grass to a hill,
As petals of gold to a daffodil,
As near as the sunlight is to the sod,
So near to the human heart is God.

Prayer: O God, help us to know that we are the ones sent, and enable us by your grace and power to be your disciples in our world. In the name of Jesus Christ, our Lord. Amen.

Ascension Sunday
Acts 1:6-11

When God Disappears

Like most fathers, when my children were small, I used to play a lot of games with them. There were afternoons when I attended an imaginary tea party given by a little girl. There were times when we played "horsey" and one of the kids would crawl on my back and I would give them a ride all over the house. Sometimes they would sit quietly while I read them the fascinating stories of *Green Eggs and Ham* by Dr. Seuss or "David and Goliath" from the book of Bible stories.

However, their favorite game was "Hide and Seek." Since they were small, I would pick one up under each arm and sit them down in the den. Then, I would run back to the bedroom and hide.

They would come toddling down the hall — cackling with laughter because they were playing a game. They would look in a couple of familiar hiding places and if I wasn't there, they would look at their mother and ask, "Where's daddy?"

Even though I was hidden just a few feet from them — under the bed or in the closet — they couldn't see me. I had disappeared, yet they knew I was still with them.

I suspect that this is something of how the disciples felt in that scripture passage in Acts. They were with Jesus and they were wondering if he would again restore the kingdom of Israel to its greatness. Jesus did not answer their question. He simply said, "You don't really need to know when and how everything is going to happen."

Then, he shifted the emphasis from the restoration of Israel to the transformation of their lives. He announced to them that the Holy Spirit would come upon them. He told them they would be given power to be his witnesses. He told them they would be witnesses in Jerusalem, Samaria and throughout the world.

When he had finished speaking these words, we come face to face with one of the most difficult passages in the Bible — the ascension of Jesus. Luke tells the story in very simple language as we writes: ". . . after saying this, (Jesus) was taken up to heaven as they watched him, and a cloud hid him from their sight . . ."

We are attracted to the unusual, are we not? And the story of the ascension is unusual. If we put ourselves in the place of the disciples, we would have an ancient concept of the universe. Remember everybody in those days belonged to the Flat Earth Society. They believed that the earth was flat. They believed that heaven was in the sky. They believed that hell or hades was under their feet. And they believed that they needed Jesus with them and when they needed him most, he disappeared from their sight.

Can you imagine the effect of the ascension on the disciples? Luke says, "They still had their eyes fixed on the sky."

There must have been a myriad of thoughts and feelings racing through the minds of the disciples as Jesus disappeared from their sight.There must have been fear and anxiety as they suddenly realized that he had disappeared and left them on their own. But, these feelings only lasted for a little while. Gradually, they realized that they were not alone. For some reason, they sensed that they were not alone. Jesus had dwelt among them, but now they believed that he dwelt within them. In some ways, Jesus was more real than he was before he disappeared. He was with them wherever they were, in the

Jewish courtroom, on the dusty roads as they went out into the world to tell others the good news, as they died in the Roman coliseums and as they hid in the catacombs and worshiped the risen Lord. Jesus was never more present nor more real to them than after that symbolic moment when Luke says, "... and he was taken up to heaven as they watched him, and a cloud hid him from their sight."

Today, as we look at this story of the ascension, there are a few things which I think are important.

I. When Jesus Disappeared, The Disciples Knew They Were Still Linked To Him.

Many people believe the greatest movie ever made was *Gone With The Wind*. That movie was made in 1939 and it has been recently re-released to the theaters and the quality of the picture has been enhanced with the assistance of computers. Along with the release of the movie there have been a lot of colorful stories about the lives of the actors and actresses in the "greatest movie ever made."

I read a humorous story about Clark Gable who many consider to be one of the most handsome and romantic stars to come out of Hollywood. On one occasion, he checked into a small-town hospital for an illness. Everyone was excited about having this famous actor in their hospital. However, there was one nurse that was at his bedside every time he turned over or moved. When he finally indicated that he would like to be alone so that he could sleep for a little while, she said, "Now, if you want anything at all, just pull on this cord."

Clark Gable smiled at her and said, "Thank you, my dear, but what is the cord attached to?"

The nurse smiled back and said, "Me."

At the very moment the disciples felt they needed Jesus, he disappeared into the clouds. But, they also knew that they were still linked to him. They knew they were still connected to God. They knew that Jesus may have gone away physically, but he was still with them. This sense of God's presence with them gave them a great feeling of confidence and boldness. They didn't really know what the future held, but they were convinced that they still had a relationship with the one who held the future.

I love that little story of a boy flying his kite. He has let all of his string out and the kit is flying so high it can't be seen. A man walks by and looks up in the air trying to spot the kite. He can't see it and he asked the boy, "How do you know the kite is up there?"

The boy smiles and says, "I can feel it tugging on my string."

Well, Jesus may have disappeared into the clouds, but we can still feel him tugging on the strings to our lives. We may not be able to see him, but we are still linked to him. God is present with us. God is in our lives. God is still connected to us through his love for us in Jesus Christ.

II. When Jesus Disappeared, The Disciples Were Bound Together In Faith.

I think it is important to notice that not only did the disciples feel a link to Jesus after the ascension, they also felt a bond of faith with one another. After the ascension when Jesus disappeared into the clouds, the disciples were bound together in a bond of faith that was stronger than any they had forged during the three years they had traveled together as the disciples of the Nazarene. They were bound together in faith because of their love and commitment to be the witnesses of Jesus Christ throughout the world.

In 1984, Leotine Kelly was elected as the first Black woman Bishop in the United Methodist Church. Shortly after being elected to the Episcopacy, she told about her father, who was also a Methodist minister. He was sent to a formerly all-white church in Cincinnati, Ohio. It was a beautiful old church with Gothic architecture, polished wood, magnificent stained-glass windows and a huge complex of buildings with the sanctuary, parsonage and education building occupying an entire city block.

Bishop Kelly said that under the parsonage was a huge cellar. It was a dark, dingy place full of cobwebs and shadows. Once, when they were playing in the cellar, they found a hole beside the furnace leading to the tunnel. Of course, they wanted to explore this tunnel and they went and asked permission from their father.

When he heard about the tunnel, he became excited. Together, they began exploring the tunnel and discovered that it ran over to the basement of the church and came out behind the furnace. That night when they sat around the dinner table, Leotine Kelly heard her father tell the story of the Underground Railroad. It wasn't a railroad with tracks, but it was a network for helping slaves to escape to freedom. The runaway slaves were hunted and would have been brutally punished if captured. It was against the law to help a runaway slave, but those in the Underground Railroad were willing to take the risk to help Black men, women and children escape to freedom in Canada.

She heard her father say, "Children, I want you to remember this day for us as long as you live, for today we found a station in the Underground Railroad. The greatness of this church is not in its Gothic architecture, nor its polished wood, nor its magnificent stained-glass windows. The greatness of this church is that we are bound together in faith with men and women who dared to take the risk and become involved in the mission of helping poor, frightened, run-away slaves escape to freedom.

Isn't that what a church ought to be doing? We ought to be bound together in the faith and mission of Jesus Christ in this world.

III. When Jesus Disappeared, The Disciples Were In A Spirit Of Anticipation.

After Jesus disappeared in the clouds, Luke tells us that two men in white garments said to the disciples, "Men of

Galilee, why are you standing there looking up at the sky? This Jesus who was taken from you into heaven will come back in the same way."

After the ascension, the disciples could look at the future in a different way. Instead of fear and doubt controlling their lives, they could look at the future with the anticipation of his coming again. They knew he was coming back. They knew he had not forsaken them. They knew they were not alone.

The last verses of the gospel of Luke also tell the story of the ascension. In this passage, Luke says: "... they returned to Jerusalem with great joy; and they were continually in the temple praising God ...." And why shouldn't there be great joy? There was joy and happiness in their lives as they anticipated his coming again.

Have you ever read the children's book, *The Little Prince*? In that story, the prince becomes close friends with the fox. On one occasion, they are trying to set a time for their next meeting. It is very important for the fox to set an exact meeting time and they finally agree to meet at precisely 4:00.

The little prince asks, "Why is it so important for you to know the exact time?"

The fox replies, "Oh, if you say you will come at 4:00, then I will begin to be happy at 3:00."

There was joy and happiness in the hearts of the disciples because they were anticipating his coming again. They were expecting the coming of his Holy Spirit. They believed the promise that Jesus would not leave them alone.

I was teaching a Bible class several years ago and a sweet little old lady raised her hand and asked, "Dr. Allen, do you believe in the second coming?"

"Believe in it?" I said. "I've experienced it! I've experienced the coming of God's spirit and God's love in my life."

And the good news of the gospel is that you can experience the coming of God's presence in your life. God is here. God is in our midst. God is in our hearts and minds. God is in this tragic, frightened, insecure, wonderful world of ours. God is here.

Isn't it time we started "being happy" because of God's presence with us?

Prayer: O God, help us to be aware of your presence in our lives. In Jesus' name. Amen.